THE CROSS AND OUR WITNESS

Dramas and Meditations for Lent and Easter

HARLAN F. HEIER

Augsburg   **Minneapolis**

THE CROSS AND OUR WITNESS
Dramas and Meditations for Lent and Easter

Scripture quotations unless otherwise noted are from the Revised Standard Version of the Bible, copyright © 1946, 1952, and 1971 by the Division of Christian Education of the National Council of Churches.

Cover Design: Lecy Design
Interior Design: Karen Buck

Library of Congress Cataloging-in-Publication Data

Heier, Harlan F., 1931–
    The cross and our witness: dramas and meditations for Lent and
Easter/Harlan F. Heier.
        p. cm.
    ISBN 0-8066-2509-0
    1. Lent—Meditations.   2. Lent—Drama.   3. Easter—Meditations.
4. Easter—Drama.   5. Drama in public worship.   6. Christian drama,
American.   I. Title.
BV85.H514   1990
246'.7—dc20   90-44358
                                                               CIP

The paper used in this publication meets the requirements of American National Standard for Information Sciences—Permanence of Paper for Printed Library Materials, ANSI Z329.48-1984.   ∞™

Manufactured in the U.S.A.   AF 9-2509
94   93   92   91   90   1   2   3   4   5   6   7   8   9   10

Contents

Chapter Six

Chapter Seven

Introduction

The death of Christ is the clearest expression of God's redeeming love for us. Therefore, the cross, once a sign of defeat and shame, has become a sign of victory and glory. Sin and death are no longer in control.

But the cross is not something we can clutch to ourselves. The cross is the symbol of God's love we carry with us into our world. We are called to witness, to share what we know about its victory with those we meet. That witness most often takes place in casual meetings with people in the settings of everyday life.

When we witness to the cross, we discover God always goes ahead of us, strengthening our witness and preparing the hearts of those who are strangers to God's Word. Sometimes we fail to see God and become discouraged by the enormity of the task before us. It is then we are surprised with an unexpected response to our telling of God's love.

The chancel dramas and meditations in this book are an attempt to call attention to the cross as the sign of God's presence and support in our lives and in our witness.

The dramas require little staging and can be presented in most chancels. They may be adapted to suit a variety of situations. In most instances, the characters may be either male or female by changing names and references to them. The characters and settings of each drama may be printed in the bulletin to help the congregation relate to the situation being portrayed.

While the themes of these dramas are appropriate for any season of the church year, they were written for Lent and Easter. The sixth drama and meditation were originally presented at the Service of Holy Communion on Maundy Thursday, and the seventh drama and meditation were presented at an Easter sunrise service.

The texts and sermon themes for this series were suggested in a Lenten preaching resource entitled *One in Mission—Nebraska*, edited by Pastor E. Gordon Jorgenson and distributed in 1987 to pastors of what would soon become the Nebraska Synod in the Evangelical Lutheran Church in America.

The material of this book was first presented at First Evangelical Lutheran Church, York, Nebraska. I am grateful to the members of First Lutheran Youth for their willingness to invest themselves in these dramas as an expression of their witness to the cross.

THE DRAMA
Blind, but Now I See

THE MEDITATION
*The Cross and Our Witness
in Faith*

Blind, but Now
I See

Characters

JIM MORRIS: A middle-aged man who is blind and confined to a wheelchair because of multiple sclerosis.

JACK BOYD: A young man who is studying for the ministry.

Setting

A very plain living room in an older house that has been converted into apartments. As the play begins JIM, seated in a wheelchair, is listening to a tape player. There is a knock at the door.

JIM: Come in, the door's unlocked.

JACK: Mr. Morris? (JIM *nods.*) I'm Jack Boyd. I'm a student at the Lutheran Seminary and I'm working this semester at Grace Lutheran Church. Pastor Johnson suggested I stop by to get acquainted.

JIM: I heard about you in the church news on the radio. Happy to meet you. (*They shake hands.* JIM *turns off the tape player.*) Pastor knows I enjoy visitors from the church. Please have a seat.

(JACK *sits. There is an awkward silence as* JACK *tries to think of something to say.*)

JACK: Isn't it nice to see the sun shine after the bad weather we've been having?

JIM: I'm sure it must be, but I can't see.

JACK: I'm sorry. I wasn't thinking.

JIM: That's okay! It's easy to take things like seeing sunshine for granted. But I feel the sun shining through the window and that's good, too.

JACK: I hope you don't mind if I ask some questions. I'd like to know you better. Are you married?

JIM: Yes, Gloria is at work. I hope you can come again when she's at home. She's a big help to me.

JACK: I'm sure she's a real support. I'd like to meet her. I've forgotten what Pastor said your trouble is. Is it muscular dystrophy or multiple sclerosis? I get the two confused.

JIM: It's multiple sclerosis.

JACK: How has it affected you?

JIM: I first noticed symptoms about ten years ago. For the last five years I've been confined to this wheelchair. Now my eyesight is failing. I can see where a window is or whether a light is on, but that's about all.

JACK: Wow! That must be tough!

JIM: It is. At first I was bitter. I kept saying, "Why me, Lord?" It didn't seem fair. I'd be the first to admit I'm not perfect, but I know lots of people who are worse than I am and they're not confined to a wheelchair. Again and again I asked God to heal me. When I didn't get the answer I wanted, I felt like my prayers were rubber balls hitting the ceiling and bouncing right back in my face.

JACK: I've never had anything that serious to pray about but I guess I'd get discouraged, too.

JIM: Well, I always thought I had faith, but before long I wasn't sure.

JACK: You don't seem bitter now. What happened?

JIM: Shortly after I had to start using the wheelchair I met Gloria. She's such a happy person. At first I resented that. I thought to myself, "Sure she's happy, but I wonder how happy she'd be if she had my problems." And then I learned that even though she didn't have multiple sclerosis her life hadn't been a bed of roses either.

JACK: She must be quite a person.

JIM: She is, but I'll let her tell you about her life herself. Her attitude made me curious. How could she be happy? One day I asked her about it and all she said was she knew God loved her and that was enough.

JACK: That's making faith pretty simple, isn't it?

JIM: Almost too simple for me. But it was doing the job for her. We spent hours talking about what God's love means and how it can build hope in us even when everything looks hopeless.

JACK: It sounds like you were having pretty deep discussions.

JIM: We were. Gloria told me about two passages of Scripture that have helped her. The first was the answer Paul received when he asked God to heal whatever was bothering him. Instead of performing a miracle the Lord said, "My grace is sufficient for you, for my power is made perfect in weakness."

JACK: That must be what my confirmation pastor meant when he said God sometimes answers prayer by giving us strength to bear burdens we would rather have removed.

JIM: I hadn't heard it put that way, but as I listened to Gloria, watched her deal with her hurts, and sometimes argued that I wasn't sure it made sense to believe in God, I began to realize God was giving me power in my weakness.

JACK: You mean you were improving?

JIM: Oh, no! God wasn't putting new strength into my legs or new vision into my eyes. But with God's help I could handle my problems. I still have days when I'm so down I'm surprised my wheelchair doesn't collapse from the weight on my shoulders. Gloria can tell you there are days when she wants to tell me to get lost. And I still ask God for a miracle, but now I add, "Your will be done."

JACK: That takes lots of faith.

JIM: I guess it does, but I am beginning to understand another of Gloria's favorite Bible verses. It's the one in which Peter describes the "living hope" we have because of Easter and adds, "In this (living hope) you rejoice, though now for a little while you may have to suffer various trials, so that the genuineness of your faith, more precious than gold which, though perishable is tested by fire, may redound to praise and glory and honor at the revelation of Jesus Christ."

JACK: Listening to you makes me think you're the one who should be in the ministry.

JIM: I guess I do get a little preachy sometimes, but my wheelchair is the only pulpit I'll ever occupy. And now that I trust God is with me even in my illness I'm sure God can use me wherever I am.

JACK: You're right—God has used you in these few minutes we've been talking.

JIM: What do you mean?

JACK: Do you mind if I start with a confession?

JIM: *(Smiles.)* As you can see, I don't have a confessional booth, but go ahead.

JACK: This seems ridiculous now that I've met you, but I wasn't anxious to visit you. In fact, it's taken almost two weeks to get up enough courage to come.

JIM: I don't understand.

JACK: I don't suppose you do. I thought you might expect me to explain why God has done such a terrible thing to you. I knew I couldn't do that and I don't like being put on the spot. You've helped me to see that faith in God doesn't depend on having all the answers. Instead, faith holds onto God's love even when there aren't any answers. That's exciting because my seminary studies aren't giving me all the answers and I wasn't sure I could go into the ministry without them.

JIM: I'm always ready to share my "God story." And if it's helped you, that's great!

JACK: I'm sorry I have to leave now. I'm nearly late for dinner at the cafeteria. To show you how worried I was, I saved this call for late afternoon so if you cornered me too badly I could honestly say I had to leave. But you can be sure I will be back. Shall we have a word of prayer before I leave? (JIM *nods and the two men bow their heads.*) Gracious God, we thank you that you show us your love in so many ways. You know how much we want health and happiness and contentment, but when we have sickness and sorrow and discouragement instead, help us to see and to trust your presence holding us up. In Jesus' name we pray. Amen.

(JACK *gets up and goes to shake* JIM'S *hand.*)

JIM: Thank you for coming, and come again.

JACK: I certainly will. Thank you for everything.

(JACK *exits.* JIM *turns his tape player back on.*)

The Cross and Our Witness in Faith

Blessed be the God and Father of our Lord Jesus Christ! By his great mercy we have been born anew to a living hope through the resurrection of Jesus Christ from the dead, and to an inheritance which is imperishable, undefiled, and unfading, kept in heaven for you, who by God's power are guarded through faith for a salvation ready to be revealed in the last time. In this you rejoice, though now for a little while you may have to suffer various trials, so that the genuineness of your faith, more precious than gold which though perishable is tested by fire, may redound to praise and glory and honor at the revelation of Jesus Christ. Without having seen him you love him; though you do not now see him you believe in him and rejoice with unutterable and exalted joy. As the outcome of your faith you obtain the salvation of your souls.

1 Peter 1:3-9

Christians present a variety of witnesses to the world through their faith. There are some who present faith as a cure-all. Their witness is: "If only you have enough faith, God will miraculously cure your illnesses, heal your infirmities, resolve your conflicts, make your business profitable, and so on."

Others present faith as the answer to every question. Their witness is: "If you only have enough faith, God will tell you exactly what to

do and how and when to do it, solve every dilemma you face, leave
you with no unexplained circumstances, no loose ends, and so on."

Obviously there are elements of truth in both those witnesses.
The Bible reveals God as all-powerful, all-knowing, all-loving.
Therefore, God can and sometimes does exactly what each of those
witnesses to faith proposes. If that is all there is to faith, however,
God is reduced to a very powerful magician for whom faith is the
magic word, the "abracadabra," that brings forth the desired result.
Furthermore, getting God to do what I want becomes the test of
the genuineness of my faith.

Unfortunately, most of us have known devout Christians—perhaps
family members or friends—who, like Jim in our chancel drama,
might describe their life in the words of God's warning to Noah in
the play *The Green Pastures* by Marc Connely: "Everything dat's
fastened down is comin' loose." Perhaps the good health they relied
on is taken from them, or the ties of love are broken, or the job or
the home they've loved and enjoyed is no longer possible for them.
"Everything dat's fastened down is comin' loose" and the hurts of
their lives have not been cured by faith. So far as we can see, their
faith is not at fault. In fact, in many instances their faith puts our
own to shame, so the words, "If you only have faith" are totally
inappropriate.

When we face such a person we feel a real empathy with Jack,
our seminary student. Our faith, like his, doesn't always give us easy
answers. It doesn't matter whether our theological education is lim-
ited to Sunday School in our grade school years or expanded to
seminary in our adult years. Questions like, "Why do the good suffer
and the evil prosper?" and "If God loves all people, why doesn't
God remove all hurtful things from this life?" still loom large and
threatening.

But thank God, through the cross, we are one with Peter, Paul,
and "a great cloud of witnesses" who continually point to "Jesus the
pioneer and perfecter of our faith, who for the joy that was set before
him endured the cross, despising the shame."

In his first letter Peter approaches the dilemma of faith and suffering in a manner far different from the witnesses I mentioned

earlier. To Peter, faith doesn't guarantee an absence of pain or provide an easy answer for difficulty. Instead, he sees in faith a support able to carry us through pain or difficulty. Each time faith is mentioned in this text the words associated with it imply strength and confidence—"You, who by God's power are guarded through faith. . . . the genuineness of your faith. . . . As the outcome of your faith. . . ."

Peter is writing to a suffering church, a church feeling the terrors of persecution for the faith. Into the despair of such a time he interjects the Easter gift of "a living hope" and points to "an inheritance which is imperishable, undefiled, and unfading, kept in heaven for you."

But I can imagine one of those sufferers saying, "It's wonderful to have the promise of such a gift kept for me by the vigilance of God. The treasure is safe, but what about me? I feel so unsafe, so continually threatened by evil." All that's promised, writes Peter, is "for you, who by God's power are guarded through faith for a salvation ready to be revealed in the last time." The God and Father of our Lord Jesus Christ who did not permit his Son to remain in the grave is also in charge of our defense. When God says, "Trust me," it's no con game. It's for real!

That's what Jim is discovering in the illness that has done its best to destroy every bit of dignity and self-worth he ever possessed. The torment is still there. His limbs are just as useless and his eyes just as blind after his rediscovery of God's faithfulness as they were before. But Jim is now aware God is there—loving and caring, understanding and forgiving. God is there, and Jim can begin to see his sufferings, his utter dependence on others, and the despair that gnaws at the pit of his stomach in a different light. In at least a small way he understands what Peter meant when he wrote, "In this you rejoice, though now for a little while you may have to suffer various trials, so that the genuineness of your faith, more precious than gold which though perishable is tested by fire, may redound to praise and glory and honor at the revelation of Jesus Christ." Jim isn't spared the wounds of the battle or the pains of life in a sinful world, but daily his confidence grows that God will see him through. The worst that life can throw at him will not destroy his faith, but will, like the refiner's fire, purify it. One day he will know the truth of the promise, "As the outcome of your faith you obtain the salvation of your souls."

The secret is, of course, in the object of Jim's faith—"our Lord Jesus Christ!"—of whom Peter writes, "Without having seen him you love him; though you do not now see him you believe in him and rejoice with unutterable and exalted joy."

"The cross and our witness through faith." Through the empty cross, the cross robbed of its victim by the resurrection, we are one in a faith that "is the assurance of things hoped for, the conviction of things not seen." We are one in a faith that may not lead us around our troubles but will carry us through them. We are one in a faith that may not give us an easy answer but will always give us an eternal assurance. We are one in a faith that may not bless us with gold but will withstand the refiner's fire like gold.

Blessed in that faith, may we be given the grace to be one with those who have witnessed through their faith over the centuries— Abel, Enoch, Noah, Abraham, Sarah, Isaac, Jacob, Joseph, Moses, Mary, the Evangelists, the Apostles, Peter, Paul, the Church Fathers, Luther, Jim, and those countless people known only to ourselves and God whose faith has touched our lives. What a company of faith that will be!

THE DRAMA

Strength in the Midst
of Weakness

THE MEDITATION

The Cross and Our Witness
in Power

Strength in the Midst of Weakness

Characters

GEORGE MANN: A man in his fifties who has become disillusioned with the Christian faith.

RUTH: George's wife who questions the value of faith, but is interested in learning about it.

DOUG: The married son of George and Ruth who is convinced there is nothing better than getting ahead.

KAREN: Doug's wife, who shares her husband's disdainful attitude toward religion.

HARRY: A devoted Christian, the same age as George.

HELEN: Harry's wife who shares her husband's Christian convictions.

Setting

The living room of a modest home in the Midwest where GEORGE, RUTH, and their son, DOUG, and daughter-in-law, KAREN, are about to be visited by old friends. The four are seated on stage. HARRY and HELEN approach from the rear of the audience and pause in the aisle. HELEN carries a Bible.

HELEN: I'm starting to get nervous about visiting the Manns. We've known them for years, but it's different since we started talking about Jesus and the church.

HARRY: I get nervous, too. It was easier to talk about things like the weather, our jobs, and our families.

HELEN: Are you sure we should be doing this? Neither of us is a pastor. I'm no expert on the Bible and neither are you. They ask so many questions and have so many arguments we can't answer.

HARRY: Well, we'll just have to wing it. At least they know we talk to them about our faith because we care about them. What a shame it would be if we didn't talk about something so important to us.

HELEN: I suppose you're right, but I feel uneasy.

HARRY: Well, here we are. I guess it's time to discover if God still answers prayer.

(HARRY *and* HELEN *go to the door and knock.* DOUG *answers the door.*)

DOUG: Well, look who's here, our own personal missionaries. Come in. I thought you'd given up on us.

HELEN: Oh, Doug, we've been friends too long to do that.

(HARRY *and* HELEN *shake hands all around.*)

RUTH: Please sit down. Would you like some coffee?

HELEN: I'd love some, thank you.

RUTH: Harry?

HARRY: Yes, please.

(*Everyone is seated.*)

GEORGE: Let's skip the small talk—I really want to begin where we stopped last time. You've been telling us God is loving and good. Right?

HARRY: Yes.

GEORGE: I used to believe that. When I was growing up, the preacher taught us, "If you have enough faith and pray hard enough, you'll be successful and healthy, and everything'll be fine."

HARRY: I've heard television preachers say the same thing.

GEORGE: I've been thinking about a family in the church we used to attend. Ruth, do you remember Hank and Joan? (RUTH *nods as though she already knows what* GEORGE *is going to say.*) They went to church every Sunday. And with them faith wasn't a show. They were really good people. Anyone who needed help could count on them to be right there.

HARRY: They must have been good church members.

GEORGE: They were—and good friends, too. But you wouldn't believe all the bad things that happened to them. Joan got some terrible disease and spent most of her life in bed. Then they got word that their son's plane was shot down in Vietnam and no one knows yet if he's dead or alive. Mrs. Schmidt didn't last long after that.

HELEN: That's terrible!

GEORGE: That's not all. Two days after their daughter's wedding, she was struck and killed by a drunk driver. Hank just couldn't take it all. He had a nervous breakdown and the last I knew he was wasting away in a mental hospital. Those people believed in God. They prayed. Lotta good it did them. Why wasn't God good and loving to them?

HARRY: I can't tell you why. But if it's any help, you're not the first to ask that question.

GEORGE: I have a hard time believing in God when I think of people like the Schmidts.

RUTH: It was heartbreaking to see all they went through after they'd tried so hard to please God.

HELEN: I'm sure it was. There are so many tragedies we don't understand.

DOUG: *(In a challenging voice)* But I thought faith in a loving God helped believers understand.

KAREN: It ought to be good for something.

HARRY: Faith in a loving God *does* help and it *is* good for something. But it doesn't protect Christians from tragedy. In the Old Testament a good man named Job lost everything. He spent days wondering why it happened to him. His religion taught him God blessed good people with riches, a large family, and good health, so it appeared Job wasn't good at all. Job's wife told him to curse God and die—in other words, get it over with. His friends told him to admit his sin. Maybe God would forgive him and give back what he'd lost.

DOUG: Blessing good people with riches, children, and good health certainly sounds more fair than what happened to the Schmidts. What's the rest of Job's story?

HARRY: Well, Job wasn't about to curse God and die. It seemed God was unfair or abandoning him, but Job considered faith in God too important to be given up easily. Job knew he wasn't perfect, but he also knew he was the same man he was before the tragedies happened. As far as Job was concerned no special wickedness had triggered his misfortunes. Instead of confessing Job argued with God about how unfair God was being.

DOUG: Good for Job!

HARRY: God let Job have his say. When Job finished, God asked what qualified him to be God's critic or adviser. Job had no answer. When God finished, Job declared anew his faith in God. Helen, could you find that passage? I think it's in the forty-second chapter.

HELEN: *(Opens her Bible to Job 42:1-6.)* Here it is. "Then Job answered the Lord. 'I know, Lord, that you are all powerful; that you can do everything you want. You ask how I dare question your wisdom when I am so very ignorant. I talked about things I did not understand, about marvels too great for me to know. You told me to listen while you spoke and to try to answer your questions. Then I knew only what others had told me, but now I have seen you with my own eyes. So I am ashamed of all I have said and repent in dust and ashes.' "

DOUG: That's just like you Christians—dragging out the Bible and reading from it like an answer book. I don't know much about the Bible but I do know Job wasn't a Christian. Besides, I don't know what he has to do with the Schmidts and their troubles.

HELEN: As a matter of fact, I was about to read another passage that sounds like Job sees Jesus and his blessings in the future. *(Opens her Bible to Job 19:25-27b.)* "For I know that my Redeemer lives, and at last he will stand upon the earth; and after my skin has been thus destroyed, then from my flesh I shall see God, whom I shall see on my side, and my eyes shall behold, and not another."

DOUG: I can't believe it! That's still worse! People should just put up with their troubles here on earth because things are going to be so wonderful after they die. That's nothing but "pie in the sky, by and by." No wonder Karl Marx called religion "the opiate of the masses." It's nothing but a drug to keep people subdued and willing to put up with all kinds of injustice. That may be okay for you, but I'm going to work hard and get what's coming to me here.

GEORGE: Besides, I remember my grandmother reading the story of Job and in the end Job gets back more than he'd lost. The Schmidts got nothing back. Hank's still suffering the torments of hell because of what he's been through. And I still want to know why!

HARRY: I can't tell you why. Job doesn't get an answer either. But because of his confidence in God, Job learns he can live with the question.

RUTH: It's strange an all-knowing, all-powerful, and all-loving God doesn't remove tragedy from the lives of those who are believers. God must know how badly people hurt. Doesn't he have the power to remove tragedy? Or doesn't he love people enough to do it?

HELEN: It may seem strange, but my belief in that all-knowing, all-powerful, all-loving God keeps me going.

HARRY: Me, too.

RUTH: I don't see how.

(There's an uncomfortable pause as though no one knows what to say. Then HARRY rises and goes over to GEORGE'S chair.)

HARRY: We really need to go. I'm sorry we don't have the answers to your questions. (GEORGE *rises and the men shake hands.*) Good night, George.

HELEN: (HELEN *and* RUTH *rise and shake hands.*) Good night, Ruth. Thanks for the coffee.

(Handshakes and good-byes are exchanged with DOUG *and* KAREN. *The* MANN FAMILY *returns to their seats and freezes in position as* HARRY *and* HELEN *leave. Part way down the aisle* HARRY *and* HELEN *stop to discuss their visit.)*

HELEN: Oh, Harry, I feel like a failure. Reading that second passage from Job played right into Doug's hands. He didn't waste a minute calling that "pie in the sky."

HARRY: I was no better. I wanted to give them answers, but I'm not sure there are any. And I wasn't going to give them "easy" answers. They've heard too many of those.

HELEN: You know, even though they are our friends, I dread the thought of going to see them again.

HARRY: I'm not anxious to go back either, but we have to. They are our friends and we care about them as much as ever. Well, let's go on home. Maybe we'll feel better in the morning.

*(*HARRY *and* HELEN *proceed down the aisle. The* MANN FAMILY *resumes their conversation.)*

DOUG: Well, I guess we showed them.

KAREN: You were great. I'd never have thought to remind them of what Karl Marx said. I bet they never come back again. If they do, I bet they don't try to tell us about their wonderful Christian faith.

RUTH: Doug, I think you were rude. I didn't bring you up to act like that. I hope they come back. And I hope they tell us more about their faith.

GEORGE: Why do you say that?

RUTH: We've been friends for so long and I want to hear more about something so important to them.

DOUG: Why do you care about their faith? It doesn't have any answers. It's useless.

RUTH: It may not have all the answers to the questions we were asking, but when I'm around Helen and Harry I feel their faith must be worth something. Doug, you were so busy putting them down you didn't notice they left with their confidence in God intact.

GEORGE: Maybe you're right. There is something different about them. I, too, hope they'll be back and I bet they will be. We've been giving them a bad time for quite a while and still they came tonight. I don't feel strong enough about many things to risk being put on the spot again and again, but they do and that impresses me.

DOUG: If they come back, you can be sure I'll be here. But I've got a hard day's work ahead of me and it's time to go to bed. Good night.

RUTH: Yes, we all need to go to bed.

(They say good night and leave the stage.)

The Cross
and Our Witness
in Power

So when they had come together, they asked him,
"Lord, will you at this time restore the kingdom of
Israel?" He said to them, "It is not for you to know
times and seasons which the Father has fixed by his
own authority. But you shall receive power when the
Holy Spirit has come upon you; and you shall be my
witnesses in Jerusalem and in all Judea and Samaria
and to the ends of the earth."

Acts 1:6-8

When I was growing up, we didn't have a lot of magazines in our
home and when *The Nebraska Farmer* or *Successful Farming* or the
Farm Journal arrived, there weren't many articles I cared to read.
But I would leaf through looking for three things—the "Song of the
Lazy Farmer," cartoons, and a particular ad. The ad that always
caught my attention featured the drawing of a really tough-looking
character. Usually he was pictured in a striped knit shirt, his rugged-
looking face sprouting several days' growth of beard, and a blackjack
sticking out of his back pocket. I was anxious to see what he was
doing, for he was always doing something completely incompatible
with his tough appearance—daintily smelling a flower, gently helping a little old lady across the street, or carefully holding the bicycle
of a child just learning to ride. The caption was always the same,
"Tough, but oh, so gentle!" I think the ad was for Perfect Circle
Piston Rings, but I'm not sure. So if any of you are willing to admit

you're as old as I am and can straighten me out on that, I'd appreciate
it.

The ad, like the chancel drama, reminds us appearances can be
deceiving. Harry and Helen appear very weak, very ineffective as
witnesses of a loving God. They can't explain how or why God
permits hurtful things to happen to his children. On the other hand,
their friends appear very strong, very effective as critics of the
Christian faith. They raise questions that seem to destroy the concept
of God as a loving Father. Even though Harry and Helen aren't
always aware of it, even though they feel like failures, they have
behind them the greatest power on earth, the very power of God,
the power promised to the disciples by Jesus in our Scripture reading: "But you shall receive power when the Holy Spirit has come
upon you; and you shall be my witnesses in Jerusalem and in all
Judea and Samaria and to the end of the earth."

The secret of the cross and our witness is power. But it is power
far different from the power we are used to seeing or using. Paul
was very aware of that difference and in the first chapter of 1 Corinthians he contrasted the power of God and the power of humans:
"For Jews demand signs and Greeks seek wisdom, but we preach
Christ crucified, a stumbling block to Jews and folly to Gentiles,
but to those who are called, both Jews and Greeks, Christ the power
of God and the wisdom of God. For the foolishness of God is wiser
than men, and the weakness of God is stronger than men." That's
important to remember. Think how often "weakness" could be written across the life and witness of the apostles to whom that power
was promised. They didn't have the power of an education, the
power of an important position, the power of great wealth, or the
power of social status. In short, they didn't have any of the powers
the world counts important. The "powers that be" were so sure of
the Apostles' weakness that they were completely comfortable treating them with scorn—sometimes driving them from town, perse-
cuting them, imprisoning them, and putting all but John to death.
Nevertheless, the power was with them. They were unafraid; they
were willing to lay down their lives that all might hear the good
news of God's love.

The fact that the apostles appear so weak reminds us that the power in witnessing is always a power not our own. In the first chapter of Romans, Paul declares the secret behind his witness: "For I am not ashamed of the gospel: it is the power of God for salvation to every one who has faith, to the Jew first and also to the Greek."

"The cross and our witness in power." What is this strange power? From the evidence of our chancel drama the power received by witnesses is obviously not a power that overwhelms nonbelievers with convincing arguments or grabs outsiders by the shirt and shakes faith into them.

Instead, the power Jesus promises is the power to whisper, "God loves you," when the world is shouting, "Hate, hate, *hate!*" It's the power that continually looks for the most winsome way possible to present God's love. It's the power that loves and cares even when those to whom the witness is given aren't particularly lovable. The power Jesus promises is the power to whisper, "I forgive you," when the world is shouting, "Revenge, revenge, *revenge!*" It's the power that remembers every one of us is forgiven much more than we'll ever be asked to forgive. The power Jesus promises is the power to whisper, "God will see you through," when the world is shouting, "Give up, give up, *give up!*" It's the power that admits it doesn't know all the answers, but still trusts the God who is always present. The power Jesus promises is the power to whisper, "God is life," when the world is shouting, "Death, death, *death!*" It's the power that looks to the fulfillment of the promise of eternal life, a life where all questions will be answered, all hurts will be healed, all tears will be dried.

"But you shall receive power when the Holy Spirit has come upon you; and you shall be my witnesses." The promise is clear. What do you suppose would happen if you and I really claimed that promise? What do you suppose would happen if we saw this verse as an assurance that we could, like Harry and Helen, share the most important thing in our lives with friends who still don't know the love and forgiveness of our God? I'm not sure many of us would suddenly feel comfortable walking into the home of a friend and saying, "I'm here to talk about my faith." But I am sure each of us would find some way to let people know whose side we're on. I'm sure each of us would find some way in our words or actions to say to people, "I love you, I really care about you, because I know God loves us both!"

That old advertisement with its slogan, "Tough, but oh, so gentle," fits us as we unite around the cross and witness in power. Critics of the church and of our own personal lives can easily, and in many instances truthfully, say we are gentle, gentle to the point of weakness, when it comes to sharing our Christian faith. How often we've almost talked to someone about God's love, but instead of joining Harry and Helen in relying on prayer and going on, we've turned back. We know our own weakness easily allows us to be driven into a corner, and that's never a comfortable place to be. But we have been promised a power, the power of the Holy Spirit, that can make us "tough" in the best sense of the word, "tough" enough to bring the force of God's word to bear in another's life.

"But you shall receive power when the Holy Spirit has come upon you; and you shall be my witnesses in Jerusalem and in all Judea and Samaria and to the end of the earth." "The cross and our witness in power." May you and I diligently seek ways to use that power among our families, our friends, and even our enemies.

THE DRAMA

Hope in the Midst of Hopelessness

THE MEDITATION

The Cross and Our Witness through Hope

Hope in the Midst of Hopelessness

Characters

LISA: A leader in the youth group.

BRENT: A member of the high school football team.

SUSIE: A popular high school girl who jokes around a lot.

JEFF: A student whose studies do not get first priority.

KARLA: A young woman who serves as sponsor for the group.

Setting

The youth room of a church on a Sunday evening where several young people have gathered around a table for devotions and a lesson. As the play begins, a lot of good-natured teasing is going on.

LISA: Do you know if anyone else is coming tonight?

BRENT: Well, Jeff said he was coming, but he'll probably be late again. He has a hard time tearing himself away from the TV.

SUSIE: I tried to talk Amy into coming, but the lucky girl has a date tonight.

KARLA: It's past time for our meeting to start so I'm going to begin with a prayer and a passage of Scripture.

SUSIE: *(Laughing)* For a change.

LISA: Shh, Susie, be serious.

SUSIE: *(Looking sheepish)* I'm sorry.

KARLA: Let us pray. Lord, you know the deep places through which our lives must go: Help us, when we enter them, to lift our hearts to you, to be patient when we are afflicted, to be humble when we are in distress. Grant that the hope of your mercy may never fail us, and the sense of your loving kindness may never be clouded nor hidden from our eyes; through Jesus Christ, your Son, our Lord. Amen.

Our Scripture lesson tonight is from the fifth chapter of Romans, beginning with the first verse: "Therefore, since we are justified by faith, we have peace with God through our Lord Jesus Christ. Through him we have obtained access to this grace in which we stand, and we rejoice in our hope of sharing the glory of God. More than that, we rejoice in our sufferings, knowing that suffering produces endurance, and endurance produces character, and character produces hope, and hope does not disappoint us, because God's love has been poured into our hearts through the Holy Spirit which has been given to us."

(Just as KARLA finishes reading the Scripture lesson, JEFF dashes in and takes a seat at the table.)

JEFF: Hi, everybody! Sorry I'm late.

(The others respond with "Hi.")

BRENT: I told you he'd be late.

JEFF: I just had to see the final minutes of the football game on TV. I shouldn't have bothered—my team lost on a field goal in the final seconds. Is it time for refreshments?

KARLA: Not so fast, Jeff. I'm not finished. I'd like to ask some questions about the verses I just read. Paul's writing about hope in suffering or, in other words, hope when everything looks hopeless. What's the most hopeless situation you can think of?

BRENT: Jeff being on time for a Youth Group meeting.

SUSIE: I know a better one. All our athletic teams beating East High in the same season.

KARLA: Those sound pretty hopeless, but I'm sure you know I'm thinking about more serious things than that. What could happen to make it difficult for you to continue to hope?

SUSIE: Please don't laugh. I know I'm not that great-looking now, but if I were in a terrible accident or something and was scarred and ugly, I don't think I could handle that. Then I'd feel really hopeless.

BRENT: I know what you mean. Playing sports is really important to me. If something happened and I wound up in a wheelchair for the rest of my life, I'm not sure I'd want to live. I don't think I could be dependent on other people for everything.

KARLA: How about you, Jeff?

JEFF: That's like when I go to the nursing home to visit my great-aunt. She doesn't know who I am or even who *she* is half the time. It's really sad. She was always so great and I know sometimes she's with it just enough to know that something's wrong. My mom and dad get really upset and are always saying what a hopeless situation it is.

KARLA: Lisa, you've been very quiet. What seems most hopeless to you?

LISA: Maybe it's because I've had a serious illness, but it seems to me death is the most hopeless thing there is. The things you've mentioned are also pretty hopeless. But even when the chances for walking again or looking normal are pretty bad, there's always a little bit of hope. But when someone dies, there's no hope. That's why people say, "Where there's life, there's hope."

KARLA: You've done a great job of describing hopeless situations. In the Scripture I read, Paul describes hope—specifically hope in the midst of suffering or hope in situations that could be considered hopeless. If we didn't know something about Paul's life, it would be easy to say, "Of course, Paul can talk about hope. He probably didn't have a bad day in his whole life." But from his second letter to the Corinthians we know Paul had lots of bad days. In a sketchy autobiography he lists imprisonments, beatings to the point of death, stonings, shipwreck, dangers from a variety of peoples, and his worry about the church. Paul could very easily feel life is hopeless, but he doesn't. What do you see as the basis for Paul's hope?

JEFF: Didn't he write something about a kind of chain reaction of suffering and endurance and character and hope?

KARLA: Yes, he did. He says each in turn produces the next.

JEFF: That doesn't sound very helpful to me. It sounds a little like "eat it; it's good for you." If I'm hurting, I have a hard time telling myself it's good for me.

BRENT: I agree with you, Jeff. When I'm in the middle of something bad, it's hard to imagine anything good coming out of it. But I've had times when after the bad thing was past I looked back and realized there was something good about it.

LISA: So have I. Those two weeks last year when I was in the hospital were bad, but later I realized they taught me to enjoy every day. I suppose those days even gave me hope because if I ever have a problem like that again I'll remember I made it through once.

SUSIE: But isn't there more to hope than our experiences?

KARLA: I think so and I believe Paul is trying to tell us that, too. Do you remember anything from the Scripture passage that might indicate that, Susie?

SUSIE: Well, I remember Paul writing, "hope doesn't disappoint us." That caught my attention because I've had times when I've been disappointed by hopes that didn't come true. So he must be talking about hope that's outside ourselves.

KARLA: You're right. Paul continues that sentence with, "because God's love has been poured into our hearts through the Holy Spirit which has been given to us." So the hope Paul's writing about is based on God's love. Now let's think back to the situations each of you described as hopeless. How can God's love in that situation turn hopelessness into hope? Susie, how might that happen if something made you feel you were ugly?

SUSIE: I'm not sure but maybe I wouldn't worry so much about how other people saw me if I was sure about God's love. God would see me for what I was—would find beauty in me—and maybe that would help me realize that other people would still find me beautiful too, only not in an outward way, of course.

KARLA: Good. Things wouldn't seem quite so black and hopeless then, would they? Jeff, how about your hopeless situation?

JEFF: That's a tough one. My first thought is my situation will stay hopeless because I'm confused and can't even remember God loves me. But there must be more to it than that.

KARLA: Can anyone help Jeff?

LISA: The only thing I can think of is something the pastor said in her sermon a few Sundays ago. I can't remember her exact words but it was something about being saved doesn't depend on how saved we feel. Do any of you remember that?

BRENT. Yeah, I think she was making the point that even when we feel abandoned by God, God is still there to stand by us and hold us up. But I'm not sure how that fits into our question.

JEFF: I think it fits. Maybe hope comes into the picture because God loves me even when I forget about God. That must be it. I still love my great-aunt when she can't remember my name.

KARLA: That may not seem like much, but it's a ray of hope, isn't it? Brent, we haven't heard from you yet.

BRENT: I guess my hope would come from something similar to Susie's. Even if I were helpless God in his love would still see something valuable in me. And God would continue to care for me and about me just like the people who love me would.

KARLA: God's love really does make a difference, doesn't it? Lisa, can you see hope in the hopelessness you described?

LISA: Yes. And it's strange. Until we bring God's love into the picture, death seems the most hopeless thing that can happen to us. But with God's love there is hope. God's love doesn't end at death. The promise of Jesus, "In my Father's house are many mansions," and his own resurrection show us that.

KARLA: Paul tells us God's love produces hope and together we've seen how that happens even in hopeless situations. Thanks for helping with this study. Does anyone have anything more to add?

JEFF: Yeah, let's go to the kitchen and eat. I'm starved.

(Amid a chorus of "Yeah," "Let's do it," the group leaves the chancel.)

The Cross and Our Witness through Hope

> Therefore, since we are justified by faith, we have
> peace with God through our Lord Jesus Christ.
> Through him we have obtained access to this grace in
> which we stand, and we rejoice in our hope of sharing
> the glory of God. More than that, we rejoice in our
> sufferings, knowing that suffering produces endurance,
> and endurance produces character, and character
> produces hope, and hope does not disappoint us,
> because God's love has been poured into our hearts
> through the Holy Spirit which has been given to us.
>
> *Romans 5:1-5*

I hope you will take a moment to do what the young people in the chancel drama did, to imagine the most hopeless situation you could experience. Or, to make it even more realistic, to recall the most hopeless situation you have ever experienced.

I suppose death is for many of us the most hopeless situation we can imagine. But there are times when we recognize there is such a thing as "a fate worse than death." As Christians we often stand more in fear and dread of the experiences that accompany death than of death itself. For example, it's natural to dread the pain and suffering, the possibility of being a vegetable, the good-byes that seem so final, the tasks that remain undone, the differences that remain unresolved, the words of gratitude that remain unspoken.

At the same time each of the other situations imagined by the young people is heavy with its own brand of hopelessness. No one wants to be a person subject to the ridicule or pity of others, a person totally dependent upon someone else, a person unable to make his or her own decisions.

When I think of a hopeless situation, I think of something that would make it even more desperate. What if a person had to face a hopeless situation absolutely alone? For example, can you imagine anyone required to bear the sorrows of death alone? Such a person would have no one to shed a sympathetic tear, no one to speak a comforting word, no one to offer a supportive presence, no one to help with the countless details. Surely that person would, out of all sorrowing humanity, be the most desolate. In fact, we would wonder how such a person could endure the dark hour of bidding farewell to a loved one. The value of the presence and sympathy of another person when we are in any crisis can hardly be overrated.

During Lent our eyes are turned in remembrance to Calvary and to the One whose situation seems hopeless as he hangs on the cross. There is a point when the hopelessness of Jesus seems absolute. As we watch him there we see him caring so completely for the needs of others—praying for the very people responsible for his crucifixion, promising a place in paradise for the penitent thief, and commending his mother, Mary, and his beloved disciple John to one another's love and concern. Then his own despair and need for some sign of hope overwhelm him, and he cries, " '*Eli, Eli, lama sabachthani?*' that is, 'My God, my God, why hast thou forsaken me?' "

Perhaps John and Mary and the other women who followed Jesus to Calvary have already fled the darkness and the earthquake, and there is no sympathetic face to which Jesus can turn. Perhaps the penitent thief is so engrossed in his own agony he has no sympathy to spare for a fellow-sufferer. Perhaps human solace is simply inadequate, and Jesus longs for the assurance of God's presence and the hope that presence can bring.

Whatever has happened, he cries out his hopeless question. The punishment of sin and death he is bearing for us has wiped out every trace of hope.

Knowing what Jesus is experiencing in that moment is in itself no comfort. But you and I, as Paul Harvey would say, "know the rest of the story." Even though at that moment Jesus is too over-whelmed to see God or feel God's supportive presence, the Father has not abandoned his obedient Son. Near the end of Jesus' ordeal God's presence in his hopelessness becomes apparent even to Jesus. He prays, "Father, into your hands I commit my spirit," and entrusts himself into the loving arms of the God of eternity. On Easter morning hope in the midst of hopelessness becomes apparent to the disciples and, through their witness, to believers of every generation, for the Crucified, abandoned to the hopelessness of death, has been raised to a living hope.

Faith in the God who rescued Jesus from death, of course, is the answer to the final question: What might make a hopeless situation more bearable? In our lesson for this meditation Paul was not just whistling in the dark when he wrote, "More than that, we rejoice in our sufferings, knowing that suffering produces endurance, and endurance produces character, and character produces hope, and hope does not disappoint us, because God's love has been poured into our hearts." Paul knew as well as we do that the cycle he was describing isn't automatic. In some people suffering produces anger, and anger produces bitterness, and bitterness produces despair. The difference comes from the last phrase of Paul's words, "because God's love has been poured into our hearts." It is in God and his love that Christians find their hope.

That doesn't mean we're never going to have times when we feel abandoned by hope. Even Paul admits his limitations when it comes to trying to understand the mystery of God's ways with his children. In the letter to the Romans he declares: "O the depth of the riches and wisdom and knowledge of God! How unsearchable are his judg-ments and how inscrutable his ways! 'For who has known the mind of the Lord, or who has been his counselor?' 'Or who has given a gift to him that he might be repaid?' "

Nevertheless, it is the same Paul who declares the confidence with which Christians can face situations that without God would be hopeless when he writes, "For I am sure that neither death, nor life, nor angels, nor principalities, nor things present, nor things to come, nor powers, nor height, nor depth, nor anything else in all creation, will be able to separate us from the love of God in Christ Jesus our Lord."

What Paul is describing is the peace and hope of knowing whose we are, of knowing to whom we belong. Believing in this God of love gives us a whole new perspective. With the author of Hebrews we can declare, "Now faith is the assurance of things hoped for, the conviction of things not seen."

The things that make us feel anxious and hopeless are many and varied. Sickness, needs beyond our resources, responsibilities, dependency, frustration, and sorrows are a few of the things that attack our sense of well-being and, therefore, our hope.

The things that offer us hope are also many and varied. Medicines to cure our sicknesses, additional financial resources, sharing our responsibilities, a sense of independence, and joy are a few of the things that build our sense of well-being and, therefore, our hope.

However, a problem arises when the forces of hope within us are overcome by the forces of hopelessness, when there is no cure for our illnesses, no adequate money for our needs, no helper to share our responsibilities, no self-care, no relief from the sorrow of death.

In our hopelessness we are driven to our knees. There we look up to the cross of Calvary and remember that we witness through hope. On that cross the ultimates of hopelessness—sin and death—were defeated by the ultimate of hope—the Son of righteousness and Lord of life. We can witness in hope because we share a faith in Christ.

Once again it is Paul who declares the hope we offer to a hopeless world: "But we have this treasure in earthen vessels, to show that the transcendent power belongs to God and not to us. We are afflicted in every way, but not crushed; perplexed, but not driven to despair; persecuted, but not forsaken; struck down, but not destroyed. . . ."

Now we, by our words and actions can announce to those around us:

> My hope is built on nothing less
> Than Jesus' Blood and righteousness;
> No merit of my own I claim,
> But wholly lean on Jesus' name.
> On Christ, the solid rock I stand;
> All other ground is sinking sand.

THE DRAMA
> *A Winning Team*

THE MEDITATION
> *The Cross and Our Witness*
> *in a Common Life*

THE DRAMA

A Winning Team

Characters

COACH JOHNSON: A young coach who appears barely older than his players, very nervous, anxious to win.

JOE: Plays center. Tall, handsome, and self-confident—expects the team to help him be the star.

CURT: Plays forward. Anxious to impress the others with his ability.

BRAD: Plays forward. A greater asset to the team than he realizes, almost shy.

RON: Plays guard. Prides himself in the number of defensive rebounds he gets.

TIM: Plays guard. Very quick and a good defensive player.

Setting

The locker room of the local high school. The basketball team has just lost another game and is waiting for the coach. They've showered and dressed and now sit wiping their faces with towels and looking dejected. Nobody speaks. After a few seconds, the coach enters carrying a clipboard.

COACH: I guess I don't need to remind you we lost again by twenty points.

JOE: It's okay, coach, we can win the rest of our games. *(Turns to the other players.)* All you guys have to do is get me the ball every time we get it downcourt. Don't forget I was high scorer in junior high.

(During the following conversation COACH NELSON *sits and listens, occasionally acting as though he is about to get up and say something to the team. At times he shakes his head as though he can't believe what he's hearing.)*

TIM: How could we forget? You've reminded us of it every game we've played since.

BRAD: Yeah, and we're all sick of hearing about it.

RON: That's for sure! Coach, if Joe thinks he can do it all by himself, why don't you bench the rest of us for a quarter and see how he does?

BRAD: Sounds like a good idea to me.

JOE: *(Jumps up like he's ready to fight* RON *and* BRAD.*)* Wow! You guys really are jealous, aren't you? I didn't say I could win the game alone, but you can't argue with the statistics. So let's start playing like a team and get the ball inside to me. *(Sits back down.)*

TIM: It doesn't sound like you're interested in playing like a team when you expect to take every shot.

CURT: Come on, Joe! It takes more than a shooter to play the game of basketball. Did you see how I dribbled the full length of the court five times the first half? I faked those guys silly.

JOE: Your ball-handling was impressive, but you forgot to mention you missed the lay-up when you got under our basket. Do all the dribbling you want, but get me the ball.

CURT: Maybe that would be a good idea.

BRAD: Oh, great, now we've got a two-man team.

RON: Aren't you two forgetting all the rebounds I've been getting this season? At the rate I'm going, I'll probably end up with the school record.

TIM: I'm not forgetting that at all. But every time you get a rebound you end up throwing the ball out of bounds. If there were a school record for throwing the ball into the stands, you'd have broken it tonight.

JOE: Tim's right, Ron. You're great at rebounding, but you're lousy when it comes to passing. You cause more turnovers than the rest of us put together. Hey, I've got an idea. Ron, when you get a defensive rebound, hand the ball to Curt. Curt dribbles down-court, gets the ball in to me, and I'll score.

BRAD: What about Tim and me? Are we supposed to stand around and watch?

TIM: Yeah, don't forget my quickness on defense draws lots of fouls.

RON: But what good are they? Tonight you didn't make a free throw the whole game. Any time our opponent needs to foul they go after you because they know you won't make the free throw.

TIM: I'm working on it! I've just had a few bad nights!

CURT: You know, Brad, I just realized you're the best playmaker on the team. We don't often give you a chance to do that, but when we do it usually works. You keep us moving around and confusing the defense. You do a good job of spotting the open player and getting him the ball.

TIM: What do you think, Coach? Are you mad at us for losing so much?

COACH: I started to say something a few times, but decided listening was smarter—it might give me some insight into our problems as a team. And it has. I wish I could have taped what you were saying so you could hear yourselves. Each of you talked about something you do best. And you didn't do too badly in your self-evaluations. Joe is a good shooter, but he doesn't think anyone else should shoot.

JOE: I told you guys to get me the ball.

COACH: Joe, be quiet and listen. Curt is a good dribbler, but he misses easy shots. Ron's excellent on rebounds, but he's not a good ball handler. Tim's good on defense and quick enough to draw lots of fouls, but he needs to practice free throws. Brad's a good play-maker, but everyone else is so busy doing his own thing he doesn't get a chance to set up many plays. And that's the key to the problem. Each of you only wants to see and use his own abilities and you forget there are four other players able to help. Right now you're not a team. You're five basketball players. Each of you has at least one special skill. If you really worked together our team would be much more than the sum of its parts. And playing basketball would be fun again.

CURT: I think I see what you're getting at, Coach.

TIM: You mean Joe was on the right track when he talked about Ron getting the rebound and handing the ball to Curt so he can dribble downcourt and pass the ball to Joe?

COACH: Only partly. He was forgetting you and Brad. He was forgetting, too, that sometimes another team member will need to rebound or dribble or pass or shoot. In other words, we need to use one another in the best way we can. That's the only way we'll win.

BRAD: It makes sense.

COACH: The five of you working together can get the job done. This reminds me of a story I read my kids recently about a kite. As the kite sailed through the air, the wind, the paper, the sticks, the string, the tail, and the boy all claimed credit for the kite's flight. Of course, not one of them but all of them flew the kite! If the wind had stopped blowing, if the paper had torn, if the sticks or string had broken, if the tail had gotten caught in a tree, or if the boy had fallen, the kite would have dropped from the sky. That might seem strange, but there's a lot of truth in it. Working together—appreciating and using one another's talents—we can do things we can never do apart. To help you remember that little story and the lesson you've learned tonight I want you to go back to the gym, run twenty staggers, and then go home and get a good night's sleep. *(Team members groan.)* Tomorrow at practice we'll work on the things we've talked about. See you then.

(Coach and team leave the stage to go to the gym.)

The Cross
and Our Witness
in a Common Life

Put on then, as God's chosen ones, holy and beloved,
compassion, kindness, lowliness, meekness, and
patience, forbearing one another and, if one has a
complaint against another, forgiving each other; as the
Lord has forgiven you, so you also must forgive. And
above all these put on love, which binds everything
together in perfect harmony. And let the peace of
Christ rule in your hearts, to which indeed you were
called in one body. And be thankful. Let the word of
Christ dwell in you richly, teach and admonish one
another in all wisdom, and sing psalms and hymns and
spiritual songs with thankfulness in your hearts to
God. And whatever you do, in word or deed, do
everything in the name of the Lord Jesus, giving
thanks to God the Father through him.

Colossians 3:12-17

What does it take to be a "winning team"? If it's an athletic team,
it's obvious the players must have talent. But from our chancel drama
it's just as obvious that five talented players do not necessarily equal
one winning team. On the other hand, avid fans of almost any sport
can point to at least one team that won far more games than the
talent of its individual players indicated it should win. In such teams
synergism occurs; that is, the effect of the whole is greater than the
sum of its parts. When those particular players play together, they

are able to support and use one another in such a way that the results are beyond what one might expect from their individual abilities.

To be a "winning team" every player must accept the oneness of the team of which he or she is a member. And part of the oneness of the team is the fact that its members share the same goal. A member of a basketball team is hardly recognizing his or her team's oneness or goal if in the middle of a game, he or she walks off the court and starts talking to a friend. Part of a team's oneness is its recognition of what it is about and what it wants to accomplish. In the case of a basketball team, the goal is obviously to play the game in such a way as to score more points than its opponent.

The lesson points to the oneness we Christians share. The Christians at Colossae are called "God's chosen ones, holy and beloved. . . ." Later in the passage Paul reminds them of the peace of Christ "to which indeed you were called in the one body."

Centuries before, the children of Israel became "God's chosen ones" through the call of Abraham. No matter how badly they forsook God and his ways God continued to consider them his chosen ones. Generation after generation God called them to be "holy and beloved." In Moses' generation that call took the form of the exodus from Egypt and the covenant established at Mt. Sinai. Later that call took the form of deliverance from a number of oppressors through judges like Gideon. Sometimes that call came through a weeping prophet, announcing a judgment he did not want to see happen. And always that call pointed to the purpose promised to Abraham, "And I will make of you a great nation, and I will bless you, . . . ; and by you all the families of the earth shall bless themselves."

Then the promised blessing of all the families of the earth happened. God's own Son, through his mother, Mary, a descendant of Abraham, became the instrument of God's call. By the sufferings and death of Jesus of Nazareth a new Israel, the church, came into being. Now the Colossian Christians and you and I are "God's chosen ones, holy and beloved." We are members of "the one body." Like the members of a winning team, we remember who we are together. As members of the church, although it is divided into many denominations, we are celebrating and looking for ways to express our unity, and we do so recognizing our oneness was given to us by God long ago. We are one not because of any particular ability or goodness we possess, but because we are loved by God.

Because of God's love for us our love for one another is part of our unity. In our text Paul writes, "And above all these put on love, which binds everything together in perfect harmony." Love for one another cancels the natural jealousy that often makes it difficult to work together. Someone has said, "It's amazing how much can be accomplished, if we don't care who gets the credit." Love honestly doesn't care who gets the credit, but rejoices instead that someone's needs are served.

As I mentioned earlier, part of the oneness of a team is its ability to set a common goal. A team doesn't exist to create a reputation for or to satisfy the whims of one or more of its players. If it does, it isn't really a team. A team exists only to accomplish the goal it is given.

As the church, you and I have already been given a goal described this way in the lesson: "And whatever you do, in word or deed, do everything in the name of the Lord Jesus Christ, giving thanks to God the Father through him."

What a privilege! Think what it would mean if the president of the United States gave us permission to use his name to accomplish our goals. We would have all the power and prestige of the presidential office at our disposal. Doors would be opened that we could never open ourselves. At the same time, what a challenge! We would have to weigh with extra consideration just what we wanted to accomplish to be sure it was worthy of the office and reputation of the president.

The president of the United States has not given us permission to use his name, but the Lord and Savior of the world has. We have the power and prestige of none less than the Son of God at our disposal. Surely that means we must put everything we do as individuals and as a congregation to the test: Is it worthy of the name of the Lord Jesus Christ? Can we submit it to him for his stamp of approval?

Much of the lesson describes attitudes and actions by which Christians can express their oneness as "God's chosen ones, holy and beloved" and can "do everything in the name of the Lord Jesus."

"Put on then . . . compassion, kindness, lowliness, meekness, and patience, forbearing one another and, if one has a complaint against another, forgiving each other; as the Lord has forgiven you, so you also must forgive. . . . And let the peace of Christ rule in your hearts . . . And be thankful. Let the word of Christ dwell in you richly, teach and admonish one another in all wisdom, and sing psalms and hymns and spiritual songs with thankfulness in your hearts to God."

In order for those things to be the rule, rather than the exception, even among Christians, two other principles from "a winning team" must be present. First of all, every player must contribute what he or she does best. As soon as the players in our chancel drama began discussing their own talents, it was obvious their abilities were not the same. Each had some things he could do to boost the chances of the team. And each had some other things he needed to avoid doing to help the team.

How often do you ask yourself, "What is it I can do best to contribute to the life of our congregation?" When you do that, please don't sell yourself short. Sometimes I think we Christians have over-learned the lesson of humility and now use it as an excuse for not having anything to contribute to our life together. Perhaps we need to remember that even the "one talent" servant in Jesus' parable was held responsible for what he did not use.

On the other side of the coin, every player on a "winning team" recognizes the contribution of the other team members, and encourages and helps them to use their abilities. At the beginning of the chancel drama Joe is willing to use his teammates, but only to help him score more points. He doesn't really see them as valuable players themselves. It's only after each player has done his best to impress the others with what he can do that Coach Johnson shows them how to turn five "hot-dogging" losers into a real team.

How often do you ask yourself, "What have I done to recognize and encourage my fellow members to 'do everything in the name of the Lord Jesus Christ?' When was the last time I spoke an encouraging and appreciative word to a Sunday school teacher, to a choir member, to a council member, to someone I saw offering loving help to another, to the pastor? Or am I more apt to stand on the sidelines and criticize so that those who are doing Christ's thing want to say to me, 'I like my way of doing church work better than your way of not doing it!' "

Our theme for this service is "the cross and our witness in a common life." No matter how separate our lives are outside the church, as a congregation we are "God's chosen ones, holy and beloved." As Christians our call is to a life bound together by God's love for us and demonstrated by our love for one another. May we accept God's challenge to be a team, sharing a common goal, contributing our abilities, and encouraging others to do the same. Only then can we "do everything in the name of the Lord Jesus Christ, giving thanks to God the Father through him."

THE DRAMA

Have a Good Day!

THE MEDITATION

The Cross and Our Witness through Service

Have a Good Day!

Characters

MARY: A pleasant, but rather calloused young woman who is a checker in a grocery store.

CATHERINE: A young woman whose clothes indicate she is poor.

JANE: A middle-aged woman who seems preoccupied and worried.

MARK: A teenager who never seems to have enough money for everything he needs.

MR. SMITH: A lonely widower whose children live out of state.

JACKIE: A wife and mother who has just learned she has cancer.

Setting

The check-out counter of a supermarket. MARY stands at the check-out counter with five customers waiting.

MARY: Next, please! (MARY *rings up a number of items on the cash register.*) That will be $3.97.

CATHERINE: (*Very quietly and ashamedly.*) I forgot to tell you I have food stamps.

MARY: *(Loud enough so everyone in the line can hear.)* Didn't you see the sign? You were supposed to tell me you were using food stamps before I started ringing up your order.

CATHERINE: I'm sorry. I haven't had to use them before and I didn't realize.

MARY: Well, I guess there isn't anything you can do about it now. Give them here! *(MARY puts the stamps in the register and hands CATHERINE her change and her receipt. Silently and sullenly she puts the groceries in a sack and hands it to CATHERINE. After a pause she remembers her boss's instructions.)* Have a good day!

(MARY and the other customers freeze in their positions at the checkout counter, CATHERINE steps to the side of the stage, carrying her groceries, and talks as though she were thinking to herself.)

CATHERINE: "Have a good day," the cashier said. I wish I could believe she meant it. "Have a good day," she said, "but don't bother me with your food stamps." She could have helped me have a good day if she'd tried to understand how it feels for someone who's always been independent and self-sufficient to have to use food stamps. I'm sure she doesn't know and probably doesn't care that my husband has been out of work for two months, but I know and I care. I work hard to let him know that even though he's unemployed I still love and respect him. I'm sure she doesn't know and probably doesn't care that my husband and I sometimes go hungry so our children have enough to eat. She said, "Have a good day," but that's pretty hard to do when I wasn't allowed to buy enough food stamps to feed our family all month. I know I'll have to ask the food bank or my church for help before the month is over. She certainly didn't help my day. I saw how the rest of the people in the line looked at me when she made a public announcement of the fact that I was using food stamps. I'm sure every one of them thinks my husband and I are lazy and good for nothing, that we've never done anything but collect on welfare all our lives. That's not true, but what good does it do for me to know that when no one believes it? I really wish I could "have a good day"—even a little sympathy and understanding could make that possible.

(CATHERINE *leaves the stage and the dialogue continues at the checkout counter.*)

MARY: Next, please! *(Rings up a number of items on the cash register.)* That will be $25.47.

JANE: *(Looks through her purse for her money.)* Oh, dear, I've forgotten my money. I can't seem to remember anything these days. I'll have to write a check.

(MARY *sacks the groceries and then stands impatiently as she waits for* JANE *to write a check. After* JANE *hands her the check,* MARY *hands her the receipt.*)

MARY: Have a good day!

(MARY *and the other customers freeze in their position at the checkout counter.* JANE *steps to the side of the stage, carrying her groceries, and talks as though she were thinking to herself.*)

JANE: Have a good day! Does she really care what kind of a day I have? Would it make any difference to her if she knew what kind of a day I've already had? . . . that I got a letter from my son yesterday, saying he and his wife are getting a divorce? . . . that I was so worried about the whole mess I didn't sleep at all last night? . . . that I can't even talk about it with my husband because he's so angry with our daughter-in-law he goes into a rage every time I bring up the subject? I have so many feelings stirring around inside myself. I worry about the grandchildren. I wonder how they're adjusting to not having their dad with them. I feel so helpless because I'm too far away to be able to do anything to help any of them. I can't even help my son move out of the house or give the grandchildren the extra hugs I know they need right now.

I feel guilty. I wonder why I didn't see they were having trouble in time to help them work it through. I wonder if there was something I failed to do in rearing my son, something that might have helped him do a better job of accepting the responsibilities of marriage and a family. And I feel angry—angry that my own child and his troubles are upsetting my comfortable little world. Yes, Ma'am, I'd sure like to "have a good day," but four little words aren't going to make it happen.

(JANE *leaves the stage and the dialogue continues at the checkout counter.*)

MARY: Next, please!

(MARK *steps up to the checkout and gives the checker a package of notebook paper.*)

MARY: *(Speaks sarcastically as though one item were not worth the bother.)* Did you find everything you need?

MARK: *(Looks over his shoulder nervously.)* Yes, I did.

MARY: (MARY *rings up the purchase.*) That'll be 97 cents.

(After MARK *hands her a dollar bill,* MARY *puts it in the cash register and hands* MARK *his receipt.*)

MARY: Have a good day!

(MARY *and the customers freeze in their positions at the checkout counter.* MARK *steps to the side of the stage, carrying his notebook paper, and talks as though thinking to himself.*)

MARK: "Have a good day!" I'd like to say to her, "Lady, if you really meant that you wouldn't treat me like I was a waste of time because I don't buy twenty dollars worth of groceries every time I come in the store." If she weren't so snotty, always treating me like I was a nobody, maybe I wouldn't try to get things past her without paying for them. I still don't know why I do it—that candy bar and Bic pen are almost burning a hole in my pocket. I don't really need either of them, but there they are. I know stealing is wrong. I die a little every time I step to the checkout counter for fear someone has been watching and reported me to the manager. I know my folks would be embarrassed if I were arrested. By the time I get out of the store I'm sorry for what I've done. But when I see that woman and realize her attitude towards me hasn't changed, it's almost like someone else takes charge. I want to get revenge on her so I do the same thing again. I know that doesn't take away my guilt, but I just wish someone would try to understand me and what makes me tick. The day that happens I'll "have a good day."

(MARK *leaves the stage and the dialogue continues at the checkout counter.*)

MARY: Next, please! (*Rings up a number of items on the cash register.*)

MR. SMITH: (*Smiling and trying to be friendly*) Hi, Mary! How are you today?

MARY: (*Continues to ring up items as though she doesn't want to talk.*) Okay.

MR. SMITH: Isn't this a beautiful day? I just couldn't sit in my apartment on a nice day like this.

MARY: (*Continues to ring up items.*) I guess it's okay. A person can't tell too much in here.

MR. SMITH: Haven't had any company for a long time.

MARY: (*Obviously trying to hurry* MR. SMITH *along*) That's too bad. That'll be $4.53.

(MR. SMITH *looks disappointed at not being able to continue the conversation, but pays* MARY *with no further comment.*)

MARY: (*Giving* MR. SMITH *his receipt*) Have a good day!

(MARY *and the final customer freeze in their positions at the checkout counter.* MR. SMITH *steps to the side of the stage, carrying his groceries, and talks as though thinking to himself.*)

MR. SMITH: Have a good day? How can I when I have no one to share my loneliness? I didn't really need groceries today, but it was an excuse to get out of the apartment. I was hoping so much I would see someone I knew so I could visit with them for just a few minutes. But there wasn't anyone. So many of my friends have died, and many of the others live in the nursing home on the edge of town. They never get out. I don't drive anymore and it's too far for me to walk to visit them. My family comes to see me when they can, but it's not like it was when families stayed in the same community generation after generation. I've got children and grandchildren scattered all across the country, so the best I can hope for is a few days' visit while they're on vacation and a phone call once a month. How I miss Matilda! Life was good when there was someone to share it. I even had to open my Christmas presents alone this year. I'm a pretty good cook, but it's hard to cook for only one person and even harder to enjoy the food alone. I tried to talk with the cashier, but you saw what happened. She barely answered my "How are you?" and didn't take time to ask me the same question. Isn't there anyone who cares about me?

(MR. SMITH *leaves the stage and the dialogue continues at the checkout counter.*)

MARY: Next, please. (MARY *rings up items on the cash register.*) That'll be $17.93.

JACKIE: (*Distractedly digs through her purse*) Oh, dear, now where did I put my billfold? Here it is. How much did you say it is?

MARY: $17.93.

JACKIE: Oh, yes. Well, here's a $20 bill.

(MARY *sacks the groceries and gives* JACKIE *her receipt and her change. As she is doing that,* JACKIE *clears her throat a couple times as though she were going to speak.*)

JACKIE: How are you, Mary?

MARY: Fine. (*Hands* JACKIE *her groceries as though signaling the end of the conversation.*) Have a good day!

(MARY *freezes in her position at the checkout counter.* JACKIE *steps to the side of the stage, carrying her groceries, and talks as though thinking to herself.*)

JACKIE: I wonder if I'll ever have a "good day" again. I've just come from my doctor and he told me the biopsy I had done last week came back positive. Even doctors have a hard time using the word "cancer," but I knew what he meant. I realized when the doctor insisted on a biopsy, cancer was a possibility, but somehow I was sure it couldn't happen to me. Cancer is something that happens to the other person. Sure, I know lots of people—more and more people, too many people—who have cancer, but not me. I wasn't prepared for that. I feel numb, like a prisoner who steps into a courtroom expecting the judge to order her to pay a small fine and being given the death penalty instead. Of course, the doctor tried to give me hope. He's recommending surgery, followed by radiation therapy, but I've heard so many bad things about radiation it's scary. I've heard I'll probably be sick to my stomach and lose my hair. All in all, I wonder if it's worth it. If only there were someone who would understand what I'm going through, someone I could talk to before I go home and tell my family. It will be as much of a shock to them as it was to me. I've heard Mary the checker has had a bout with cancer—if only she weren't always in such a hurry. If only she had time to help me find something good in my day or for that matter, in the rest of my life.

(JACKIE *leaves the stage.*)

MARY: Thank goodness it's finally time for me to get off work. I've had it.

(MARY *steps to the side of the stage and talks as though thinking to herself.*)

MARY: "Next, please. . . . That'll be this many dollars and that many cents. Here's your receipt. Have a good day!" Can any of those customers realize how tiresome it is saying the same thing over and over again all day? And I'm supposed to say it with a smile, even when my feet are killing me. After a while, even the customers become just one big blur passing in front of my check stand. "Have a good day," I tell them and I don't know them at all. I wish I had a million dollars so I could really help them have a good day, so I could demonstrate by some grand gift how much my Christian faith means to me. But what chance do I, a checker in a grocery store, have of being able to help someone have a "good day"?

(MARY *leaves the stage, like a person tired after her long day.*)

The Cross and Our Witness through Service

And he called to him the multitude of his disciples,
and said to them, "If any man would come after me,
let him deny himself and take up his cross and follow
me. For whoever would save his life will lose it; and
whoever loses his life for my sake and the gospel's will
save it. For what does it profit a man, to gain the
whole world and forfeit his life? For what can a man
give in return for his life? For whoever is ashamed of
me and of my words in this adulterous and sinful
generation, of him will the Son of man also be
ashamed, when he comes in the glory of his Father
with the holy angels."

Mark 8:34-38

In his book, *Key Next Door*, Leslie Weatherhead tells a true story
that illustrates service that is literally sacrificial. Centuries ago, For-
mosa, now known as Taiwan, was governed by a Chinese governor
named Goho. Goho was a man of humane and liberal outlook, and
one of the things he did when he became governor was to induce
the savage tribes under his rule to abandon the custom of human
sacrifice. He persuaded them to be content instead with an ox or a
pig as their victim. For forty years this continued. But at last, after
an unusually bad harvest, the leaders of the people came to him
and said this would never do; their gods were angry, and now they
must have a human victim once again. Goho reasoned and pleaded

69

with them, but in vain. Finally, seeing that he wasn't going to convince them, Goho gave in. "Go," he said, "tomorrow morning to such and such a place in the forest, and you will find the victim ready—a man tied to a tree, wearing the red robe of sacrifice and a red cloth over his face and head. Strike! for he is your victim."

The next morning the men gathered at the appointed place, and there they saw the victim dressed in red, his face covered with a red cloth. In a frenzy they rushed upon him, and struck off his head. But as the cloth rolled away from it, they saw the face of the victim they had killed. It was Goho himself. From that day to this, no human sacrifice has ever been offered on the island of Taiwan. So Goho reconciled those crude savages to himself. By the sacrifice of his life he did what his rule and teaching had failed to do—he changed their whole minds, and changed them permanently.

Thereafter, a red robe became the symbol of a changed life. A man would discard his former dingy robe and wear a red one, as if to say, "I am one of Goho's men. I am different." They became known as men of the robe.

In the lesson from the Gospel of Mark, Jesus commends to us service that is sacrificial in a broader sense, service by which we deny ourselves in order to be free to serve others in his name. He says, "If any man would come after me, let him deny himself and take up his cross and follow me. For whoever would save his life will lose it; and whoever loses his life for my sake and the gospel's will save it."

The chancel drama highlights that teaching by way of contrast. The people in the drama are wrapped up in themselves and, considering the load each person is carrying, that's not surprising. Each person is trying to save himself or herself, refusing to be spent or lost in service to another.

Each of the customers in turn doubts the sincerity of Mary the checker and her almost mechanical "Have a good day!" Instead of "a good day," the young woman who must use food stamps because of her husband's unemployment gets scorn. Instead of "a good day," the lady whose son's problems cause her to be forgetful gets impatience. Instead of "a good day," the young man who shoplifts to get even with the checker's rudeness gets a guilty conscience. Instead of "a good day," the lonely man who hopes for just a few minutes of conversation gets a "bum's rush." Instead of "a good day," the woman who has just learned she has cancer gets indifference. But in the end we are forced to recognize that none of the customers reaches out to help Mary have "a good day" either.

Years ago I saw a little pamphlet entitled, "A man wrapped up in himself makes a mighty small package!" I don't remember anything about the pamphlet except its title. But that's such an obvious truth I've never forgotten it. How easily we shrink our world until it no longer reaches beyond ourselves and our needs! When that happens we become blind to the needs and hurts of others. And we betray the dominion of Jesus Christ in our lives.

The only way we can break out of that "mighty small package" is to remember Jesus' words and look to his life and ministry, death and resurrection for a demonstration of what that means. Again and again in his earthly ministry he spent himself in caring love for those around him. Even on the cross he prayed for those who had brought him to the crucifixion. He welcomed a repentant sinner into his kingdom. He provided for his mother and his best friend. And he did it all before he expressed any of the needs he himself was experiencing. It's no wonder that love draws us from ourselves to him.

Relying upon that kind of love, we realize Christian service isn't always a money matter. Jesus didn't have wealth or influence, but he used what he had and what he was to support those whose lives touched his. The chancel drama underlines that truth by way of contrast. Mary chooses to forget it doesn't take "a million dollars" to demonstrate by some grand gift how much her Christian faith means to her. Later, in describing the conditions of discipleship, Jesus says, "For truly, I say to you, whoever gives you a cup of water to drink because you bear the name of Christ, will by no means lose his reward." For the group of customers who have just passed through Mary's check stand the "cup of water to drink" might have been a friendly smile, a bit of sympathy for people who must use food stamps, a sensitivity to people who are distracted by worry, an expression of understanding and concern for the difficulties of teen-agers, and a few extra words for people who are lonely.

But we can understand Mary's feelings. How many times we've thought to ourselves, "If only I were rich, I'd certainly be generous!" How easily we excuse ourselves from serving others because we can't make the big gift! At least we can't make it without self-denial or sacrifice. But that's exactly what Jesus is asking of us in our text. We'll never give even "a cup of water to drink" if we're continually worrying whether our thirsts will be met. We'll never take time to let people know we care, really care about them, if we're continually worrying what our caring might cost us or whether we're going to have enough time for ourselves.

"The cross and our witness through service!" "If any man would come after me, let him deny himself and take up his cross and follow me. For whoever would save his life will lose it; and whoever loses his life for my sake and the gospel's will save it." The Moravian Church has a symbol that is a good expression of two possible ways in which these words of Jesus can be understood. In the center of the symbol is an ox. On one side is a plow and on the other is an altar. Underneath are the words, "Ready for either." Even in our day there are Christians whose service is a martyr's death. But the service of the vast majority is by way of the plow, doing the daily tasks of serving love that often seem more dull and tiresome than exciting and dangerous.

As you and I stand at the foot of the cross, I'm not suggesting we abandon the wish, "Have a good day!" Instead I'm suggesting we fill it with meaning by asking ourselves, "How can I help the recipient of my wish have a good day? Is there some loving service I can offer to show something of the love of Christ that literally denied itself and took up a cross that we might live?" In that kind of willingness to be spent each of us and the persons whom we serve in Christ's name will have a better day!

THE DRAMA
You Have Been Chosen

THE MEDITATION
The Cross and Our Witness through a Calling

You Have Been Chosen

Characters

JULIE GORDON: A vivacious, enthusiastic middle-aged woman.

HANK GORDON: Julie's husband, more down-to-earth and skeptical.

Setting

A living room in a modest home just after the occupants have been notified they have been given a free trip to Hawaii. HANK is comfortably seated, but JULIE is pacing up and down the room, waving a letter in her hand.

JULIE: Can you believe this—a ten-day trip to Hawaii and it's all ours *free*? I've always wanted to visit Hawaii and now we're going to do it.

HANK: I don't know, Julie. Have you read all the fine print? There's bound to be a catch someplace.

JULIE: No, Hank, there's no fine print. It's all very plain and simple. (*Reading the letter.*) "Dear Mrs. Gordon: Congratulations! You and your husband have been chosen by a friend to receive a ten-day all-expense paid trip to Hawaii. The trip includes air travel from your home town, a room at the Sheraton Princess Kaiulani Hotel, transportation and meals while on the islands, and $200 spending money. Arrangements have been made for you to receive your tickets through our agency. Please call us at ATR-AVEL (287-2835) for information about flights and hotel reservations that would be convenient for you. Sincerely, Betty L. Jones, Travel Coordinator, Ace Travel Agency."

HANK: But you know what the Better Business Bureau says, "If it sounds too good to be true, it probably is." And if anything ever sounded too good to be true, this does.

JULIE: Just think of all the sightseeing we'll be able to do. It's a dream come true. The only time we've been out of the state was when we went to Denver on our honeymoon, and then you could only get three days off work. We drove five hours after our wedding reception going out and all night coming home just so we'd have some extra time in the mountains. It was really tiring.

HANK: I know. I sure couldn't handle that much night driving now and your snoring wouldn't help keep me awake either.

JULIE: Oh, come on now, I don't sleep that much when we drive. Remember how we came back from that trip certain we wanted to see more of the world? But we've never been able to do it.

HANK: How could I forget? Every time we got a little money put aside for travel one of the kids needed braces on their teeth or glasses, or the house needed a new roof or a new furnace.

JULIE: But now we can travel—not just to the next state, but all the way to Hawaii! You won't have to drive—air fare and transportation on the islands is provided. And we won't be camping. "The Sheraton Princess Kaiulani Hotel"—doesn't that have a romantic and exciting ring to it?

HANK: And you won't have to cook! Doggone it! Your enthusiasm is catching. I just hope you're not getting your hopes up too high.

Are you sure it doesn't say, "This trip is yours as soon as you agree in writing to be my slave the rest of your life?"

JULIE: No, Hank, I've read this letter so often I practically have it memorized.

HANK: But, let's be practical. Who would give us a free trip to Hawaii? We don't have any rich friends. And even if we did, why would they do that for us? It would be more natural for them to spend the money on themselves.

JULIE: Well, I have to admit I haven't been able to think of a single person who could or would do that. I was hoping you might think of someone, perhaps someone we'd done a big favor for.

HANK: I can't. I hate to say this, Julie, but it seems to me this letter is a hoax—a cruel hoax.

JULIE: Oh, Hank, it just can't be. Look, the stationery looks genuine.

HANK: Almost anyone could get a piece of stationery from a travel agency. Now think about it, have you ever met "Betty L. Jones"?

JULIE: No, but . . .

HANK: Well, neither have I. And it sure wouldn't take a very active imagination to make up a name like that.

JULIE: That's true, but I can't imagine anyone carrying a practical joke that far. Our friends all know about my wish to visit Hawaii and—

HANK: *(Interrupting)* That's it. Every one of them knows you want to go to Hawaii so badly you'd fall hook, line, and sinker for this fool letter. There's probably a group of them together tonight laughing about what fools we are.

JULIE: Oh, Hank, I can't think of a friend who would give us such a valuable gift, but neither can I think of anyone who would be cruel enough to pull this kind of practical joke on us.

HANK: I have to admit, I can't either.

JULIE: You see, it may be true after all. Please let me dream about this wonderful trip tonight.

HANK: Well, okay. But don't get your hopes up too high because the first thing tomorrow I'm going to call the Ace Travel Agency, ask for Betty Jones, and get to the bottom of this.

JULIE: It's a deal. I don't know why I didn't think of that this afternoon when the letter came. I was so sure it was true that all I could think about was what a fun time we would have. But let's go to bed. Even if the letter's a hoax, I don't want to miss a minute of that dream.

(HANK *and* JULIE *leave the stage.*)

The Cross and Our Witness through a Calling

> But you are a chosen race, a royal priesthood, a holy
> nation, God's own people, that you may declare the
> wonderful deeds of him who called you out of darkness
> into his marvelous light. Once you were no people but
> now you are God's people; once you had not received
> mercy but now you have received mercy.
>
> *1 Peter 2:9-10*

Can you imagine yourself in the position of the couple in our chancel
drama? You are asked to believe, and really want to believe, something that by all logical thought is too good to be true. What a
contrast between what had been and what will be—if only you can
believe the gift! Before you've not even been able to put together
enough money to travel to the next state and camp; now you're
given the privilege of traveling to Hawaii and staying in a luxury
hotel. But there is a certain risk in believing the gift offered in the
letter—if someone is playing a trick, you'll end up making a fool of
yourself. And yet you can't afford to ignore the offer. To do that
would be to make another kind of fool of yourself. If you're going
to receive what is offered, you have to place a certain amount of
faith in the genuineness of the letter you've received and in the
integrity of one "Betty L. Jones" whom you've never met. That's
not an easy thing to do.

Now come with me from that living room to the upper room in
Jerusalem that first Maundy Thursday. The apostles have gathered

to celebrate the Passover with Jesus. In the midst of lessons on humility and love, predictions of his going away, and promises about the many rooms in his Father's house, Jesus takes bread, gives thanks, breaks it, and gives it to the disciples, saying, "Take and eat; this is my body, given for you." And giving them wine he says, "This cup is the new covenant in my blood, shed for you and for all people for the forgiveness of sin."

Imagine yourself as one of the apostles around the table that night. You, too, are asked to believe something that to all rational thought is too good to be true. It's only a bite of unleavened bread and a sip of wine. How can such everyday things be the body and blood of your Lord and Master? How can they be the means by which all believers will receive the forgiveness of sin? As a disciple, you know Jesus too well to suspect he's playing a trick on you. But you also know he's been under a terrible strain lately. Can the strain have caused some kind of delusion within him?

Obviously, the apostles, too, are called to believe, to be willing participants in a gift only God can give. And each is required to decide how much he is willing to risk in accepting what Jesus is promising. It's not the first time they've had to make such a decision. Nor will it be the last time. It began when Jesus said, "Come, follow me." And it will continue when he stands before them in the upper room on Easter evening and says, "Peace be with you." Because of the promise, "and lo, I am with you always, to the close of the age," they will be making such decisions the rest of their lives. In the process Jesus offers a challenge to accept what he alone can offer them, to be what he alone can help them be. And that, too, often seems a gift beyond belief.

This lesson is one of my favorite passages of Scripture. How beautifully it describes our calling as Christians: "But you are a chosen race, a royal priesthood, a holy nation, God's own people, that you may declare the wonderful deeds of him who called you out of darkness into his marvelous light. Once you were no people but now you are God's people; once you had not received mercy but now you have received mercy."

Talk about an unbelievable gift. That's a before and after story that tops our chancel drama by a mile. "Once you were no people but now you are God's people." Think how true that is. There are so many things that could keep us from being a people, that could separate us. Some of the things that separate us are obvious sins, like pride, jealousy, and indifference. Others are simply a matter of who we are as persons. Because of a variety of educational, financial, and social backgrounds, we may feel we have nothing in common or do not enjoy one another's company.

But through the power of the cross, God calls us not simply to be *a* people, individuals gathered together, but to be *God's* people, individuals gathered together around God and his love. As God's people, we are declared to be "a chosen race, a royal priesthood, a holy nation." What a success story! From nothing to all of that! There is one little catch to it, but it's a catch that's not really a burden. For Peter continues, "that you may declare the wonderful deeds of him who called you out of darkness into his marvelous light." Can you imagine Julie and Hank risking belief in the letter's promise, finding the trip as enjoyable as they had hoped, returning home, and never saying a word about the trip or how it came to be theirs? Or saying to one another, "Well, I suppose we have to tell our friends about our trip"? Every person they can possibly corner will hear about the marvelous thing that has happened to them. That's all God asks of us in return for his call and promise of love.

"The cross and our witness through our calling." God continues to call you and me through the cross to enjoy the greatest blessings possible, blessings beyond anything we could ever deserve or repay. We are called to the blessing of being a child of God, members of God's people. That's our main vocation. We are never only a farmer, a housewife, a secretary, a janitor, a pastor. We are always a *Christian* who is a farmer, a housewife, a secretary, a janitor, a pastor. As "a chosen race, a royal priesthood, a holy nation, God's own people," we can never doubt our worth to God. God is always helping us to become more and more what he has called us to be. And every prayer, every act of worship or meditation, every sharing in the Sacraments strengthens us to "declare the wonderful deeds of him who called (us) out of darkness into his marvelous light."

May God grant us the wisdom and courage to accept and live out the gift given us by his love on the cross.

THE DRAMA

The Budding of an Easter People

THE MEDITATION

The Cross and Our Witness to Easter's Promise

The Budding of an Easter People

Characters

CHARLIE: A middle-aged husband and father who attends church only when it fits his schedule.

JUNE: Charlie's wife, who enjoys church and attends more often than her husband.

SHERRY: Charlie and June's daughter who attends Sunday school and church regularly and has learned a great deal about the Christian faith.

BERNIE: Sherry's brother, who attends Sunday school and church, but doesn't take it as seriously as his sister.

Setting

The living room of an upper-middle-class home. The family is returning from the Easter service. SHERRY and BERNIE enter first. SHERRY goes to a lily sitting on an end table.

SHERRY: What happened to the lily?

BERNIE: *(Feigning innocence)* What lily?

SHERRY: This lily, of course. A blossom's missing. I bet you did something to it.

BERNIE: Not so loud.

SHERRY: What did you do, Bernie?

BERNIE: I had a little accident with my basketball. Please don't say anything. Mom'll just get upset.

SHERRY: Mom told you not to play with your basketball in the house.

BERNIE: I didn't mean to—I'm sorry. Maybe they won't notice.

SHERRY: I bet they will. Tell them. It'll probably be okay. They love you more than the lily.

BERNIE: I don't want to spoil Easter for them. *(Hears their parents coming)* Shh!

(Parents enter the room and sit on the sofa. CHARLIE is carrying the Sunday paper and immediately begins to read it.)

JUNE: That was such a beautiful service—so inspiring! Didn't you think so, Charlie?

CHARLIE: *(More interested in the newspaper than in conversation.)* Huh? Oh, yeah, I guess so.

JUNE: Easter lilies are so beautiful and I do like that smell. It just smells like Easter should smell.

CHARLIE: *(Resigning himself to the fact that his wife is not going to let him read the paper, he lays it down.)* I don't know why they fill the chancel with lilies. I think it looks cluttered. Besides, I think lilies affect my allergies. *(Reaches for handkerchief and wipes his nose.)*

SHERRY: My Sunday school teacher told us lilies are a symbol of Easter. When the lily bulb is planted it dies and a beautiful plant grows because of its death. The lily's white blossoms are symbols

of joy and glory *(with a knowing look at* BERNIE*)* . . . and innocence.

BERNIE: *(Anxious to turn the conversation away from lilies.)* How
about the choir? I thought they were great!

JUNE: The choir did sound extra good this morning. The anthem
reminded me of a song on my record by the Mormon Tabernacle
Choir. *(Turning to the children)* And I know your Dad enjoyed
the anthem. I can tell he's enjoying the anthem when he keeps
time to the music.

CHARLIE: Okay, you caught me. The choir sounded joyful this morning. They sang like they believe Easter is something to sing about.
They looked happy, they sounded happy, and they made me happy
to be there. *(He suddenly notices everyone is smiling and realizes
what they're thinking.)* But don't get the idea I'm going to church
every Sunday. After all, Sunday's my only morning to sleep in.
Besides, it's spring and it won't be long before the lawn and garden
need attention. Sunday's the only time I can take care of that. I
can tell you one thing, the place next door would look a lot better
if George used some of the time he spends at his church on lawn
care.

JUNE: You do keep our lawn looking nice.

CHARLIE: That's not all. The house needs painting and I need time
to golf. Besides, today was special. Today was Easter and not every
Sunday's Easter.

SHERRY: My Sunday school teacher would disagree with you, Dad.

CHARLIE: What do you mean, Sherry?

SHERRY: Mr. Pratt says that we Christians worship on the day when
God raised Jesus from the dead and finished our redemption. We
worship on Sunday to celebrate Easter. So if you're going to stay

home from church, you'll have to find a better excuse because every Sunday is a little Easter.

CHARLIE: I didn't remember that.

JUNE: It was too bad that little girl got lost from her parents after church.

SHERRY: Remember when I got separated from you in Gold's Department Store?

JUNE: I certainly do. You let out quite a howl!

SHERRY: You were on the other side of a rack of dresses all the time. But I didn't know. *(Laughs)* It's funny now, but I still remember how scary that was!

BERNIE: I meant to ask before. What was that beat-up old cross doing up front in church?

CHARLIE: I sure don't know. I think someone should complain to the pastor. It looked out of place next to our new altar.

SHERRY: But, Dad, there wouldn't be Easter without the cross.

CHARLIE: I know, but why such an ugly thing?

SHERRY: It's nice to have shiny crosses, but that old wooden one reminds us the cross Jesus died on was ugly and shameful. Only the worst criminals—those who murdered or tried to start a revolution—were put to death in that way. Some hung on the cross for days before they died.

BERNIE: Yeah, the cross was like our electric chair or gas chamber.

SHERRY: That's right! It was a disgrace to be crucified. But the cross at church didn't have a body hanging on it. Instead there were palm branches and Easter lilies, signs of life.

JUNE: When I looked at that cross this morning I thought about Grandma. It was a little over a year ago she died.

BERNIE: Did that make you sad?

JUNE: Yes and no. She'd been so sick. Her life wasn't like a new, shiny cross; it was like that old one. But Easter tells us everything is different for her now. Life is new and beautiful because she lives with Jesus.

SHERRY: That's why I'm glad we sang, "I Know That My Redeemer Lives." Grandma knows how true that hymn is.

CHARLIE: Sherry, I like listening to you talk about Easter. You've given it a lot of thought.

SHERRY: I have. Easter is the key to everything we believe. Jesus is alive and he wants us to know he's with us every day, not just once a year.

BERNIE: Hey, Mom, I have a confession to make. I knocked the blossom off your lily with my basketball. It was a mistake—I'm sorry.

JUNE: I was afraid that would happen and I noticed it was gone, but I wasn't going to mention it. Thanks for telling me.

SHERRY: I'm getting hungry. Is dinner ready, Mom?

JUNE: It smells like the ham is about done. If you help set the table, we'll eat soon.

BERNIE: All right! Let's go!

(Everyone leaves the stage to put the finishing touches on the Easter dinner.)

The Cross and Our Witness to Easter's Promise

Now if Christ is preached as raised from the dead, how can some of you say that there is no resurrection of the dead? But if there is no resurrection of the dead, then Christ has not been raised; if Christ has not been raised, then our preaching is in vain and your faith is in vain. We are even found to be misrepresenting God, because we testified of God that he raised Christ, whom he did not raise if it is true that the dead are not raised. If Christ has not been raised, your faith is futile and you are still in your sins. Then those also who have fallen asleep in Christ have perished. If for this life only we have hoped in Christ, we are of all men most to be pitied.

But in fact Christ has been raised from the dead, the first fruits of those who have fallen asleep. For as by a man came death, by a man has come also the resurrection of the dead. For as in Adam all die, so also in Christ shall all be made alive. But each in his own order: Christ the first fruits, then at his coming those who belong to Christ. Then comes the end, when he delivers the kingdom of God the Father after destroying every rule and every authority and power. For he must reign until he has put all his enemies under his feet. The last enemy to be destroyed is death.

1 Corinthians 15:12-26

Most of us are familiar with Hans Christian Andersen's children's story, *The Ugly Duckling*. As you may remember, the story begins with a duck hatching a nest of eggs. Surrounded by her other beautiful, yellow ducklings she waited for the last egg to hatch. And when it hatched, the bird that emerged was bigger than the others and an ugly grey. Everyone picked on him. They treated him like the ugliest duckling to ever live and he grew up believing this. But when he was fully grown, he met some majestic swans. As he swam toward them he looked into the water and saw his own reflection. He, the ugly duckling, was no longer a dark gray bird, ugly and awkward. He was a white swan, beautiful and stately like the others. The promise of beauty and grace was in him all along. Unknowingly he had become what God intended him to be. He had been readied for a new life.

I remind you of that beautiful little story because there is a sense in which the Easter experience is an "ugly duckling" story. Think of the contrasting feelings of the disciples between Maundy Thursday and Easter. It was easy to see the tension and ugliness building as they gathered with Jesus in the upper room for the Passover supper. Much to their dismay Jesus talked about "going away" and warned them a betrayer was in their midst. Later, that same evening, in the Garden of Gethsemane they stood helpless as a "great crowd with swords and clubs" took Jesus prisoner.

In the morning John brought the other disciples word that the fate of Jesus had been sealed. The Jewish officials decided he must die. It was only a matter of how and where and when. The next word was that Pilate had decreed Jesus would be crucified on Golgotha at noon. The stage was set for the ugliest, saddest, most shameful day of their lives. The false night of the eclipse matched the despair of their mood.

About sundown some of the women among the followers reported the body of Jesus had been buried in the tomb of Joseph of Arimathea. The disciples took some comfort in the burial because it meant Jesus had been spared the ultimate disgrace of having his body thrown on the town garbage heap. But it was a small comfort compared to how much they had lost by his death.

I can't imagine the disciples venturing far enough from the security of locked doors that Saturday to view the instrument of Jesus' death. But in their minds' eye the cross appeared ugly and frightening.

Toward dawn on the first day of the week, Mary Magdalene and the other Mary visited the tomb. They returned with strange babblings about an open, empty tomb, about a message from an angel, and, most puzzling of all, about meeting Jesus along the way.

The disciples weren't able to put it all together immediately. They needed time to absorb these strange reports. An empty tomb wasn't impossible. Perhaps the body of Jesus was a victim of grave robbers. Perhaps his enemies weren't satisfied with their earlier vengeance and added this last insult. Perhaps Joseph of Arimathea, or another friend, had taken Jesus' body before his enemies could desecrate it.

Because of those possibilities, even an empty tomb held little promise for the disciples. It was certainly not enough to dispel the darkness that had engulfed them the past few days. But the insistence of the women that they had seen an angel and Jesus himself was an entirely different matter. Like the slow rising of the sun on a spring day, it dawned on them that Jesus really was alive. Now everything was changed. What had been ugly with despair and death was beautiful with hope and life!

The promise of Easter had been with the apostles all along, but they hadn't been able to see it. Only when Easter becomes reality do Paul's words to the Corinthians make sense: "For the word of the cross is folly to those who are perishing, but to us who are being saved it is the power of God. . . . For Jews demand signs and Greeks seek wisdom, but we preach Christ crucified, a stumbling block to Jews and folly to Gentiles, but to those who are called, both Jews and Greeks, Christ the power of God and the wisdom of God."

The promise of Easter is the promise of "God with us." For the apostles the most disheartening factor of Good Friday was the overwhelming evidence that God had abandoned Jesus of Nazareth. If God wasn't present for the One so dedicated to love and mercy, we, like a child separated from his or her parent, can only cry out our lostness.

In spite of the black cloud of sin that hid God from view and caused the anguished cry, "My God, my God, why hast thou forsaken me?" Easter declares that Jesus was not abandoned. God was keeping watch over his own, hearing his every prayer, holding him up when he felt most beaten down.

That promise of Easter remains. Problems or successes, pains or pleasures may cause us to lose sight of God, but God never loses sight of us. The declaration of the Psalmist, "God is our refuge and strength, a very present help in trouble," was, and still is, very true.

The promise of Easter is also a promise of forgiveness. How heavily guilt weighed on Peter's mind between Good Friday and Easter. Like Bernie in our chancel drama he had been warned. With scarcely a thought, he bought a little security with a simple denial. The words, "I do not know the man," had barely left his lips when he realized what he'd done. But it was too late. In a matter of hours the death of Jesus robbed him of an opportunity to say, "I'm sorry."

Then at last the torturous hours passed, and Peter heard the news of Easter directed especially to him, "Tell the disciples and Peter." As far as Jesus was concerned, Peter's guilt didn't make him unfit to be an apostle. Instead, Jesus offered the freeing power of a forgiveness complete enough to entrust to him new responsibilities in the kingdom. Only Peter could decide whether he was willing to accept the reality of that forgiveness.

Like Bernie, you and I are sometimes not ready to claim the promise of forgiveness. And until we do, life is a matter of hiding what we are and what we've done. In the process the friendship we might have known with God disappears. Easter declares the promise of forgiveness is ready. God, our loving parent, has made his willingness to forgive known through the death and resurrection of his Son. The decision whether or not to accept belongs to us.

The promise of Easter is also a promise of life. The apostles learn Easter is more than the escape of Jesus of Nazareth from the tomb. He is not only alive; he is also life. He is life right where they are, tempted to go back to their boats and tax booths and houses and farms. He is life right where they need help to turn their lives from self to God and others, from being served to serving. With the risen

Lord at their side, they can say with Paul, "For to me to live is Christ."

Every Sunday is a little Easter; every day is also. Life in Christ is lived out as priorities are set and lives are ordered by his living presence. That's the promise toward which Charlie reaches, but to which he isn't ready to commit himself.

That brings us to the heart of the Easter promise—life eternal. That was not an easy promise for the early Christians to accept. In the Corinthian congregation there were people who accepted the truth of Easter but refused to believe in the resurrection of the dead. Paul warned that to refuse to believe that God can change the ugliness of death into the beauty of everlasting life, is also to refuse to believe that God made that change for Christ on the first Easter. Faith in Christ then is rendered meaningless.

After Paul listed these consequences, he added his own testimony to the promise of Easter, "But in fact Christ has been raised from the dead, the first fruits of those who have fallen asleep," and he finished his own credo, "For to me to live is Christ, and to die is gain." Christ is alive and June can trust Grandma enjoys that other promise, "In my Father's house are many rooms. . . . And when I go and prepare a place for you, I will come again and will take you to myself, that where I am you may be also." Christ is alive and we can entrust our loved ones to that same loving home.

The power and wisdom of God displayed through his risen Son is an Easter promise for each of us. Easter is God's promise that we can be what God planned for us to be all along. It contains the promise that he is "God with us," never considering us "ugly duck-lings"—out of place in his family. Instead God has done everything necessary to forgive us and to give us new life both here and now as well as in eternity.

What we have seen in the chancel drama is the budding of an Easter people. Like a bud, the lives of this family contain the promise of a beautiful blossom, the fullness of the blessing of God's presence and forgiveness and life. Our lives, too, are a strange mixture of the Easter promise fulfilled and unfilled. There are times when we are unwilling to admit our guilt and claim the promise of forgiveness. There are times when we recognize the promise of "God with us" even when we feel lost from God. There are times when we're too busy to commit ourselves to God. There are times when we see a loved one's new life through "the resurrection of the dead and the life everlasting."

Whether or not we accept God's Easter promise in faith, it stands forever. It's in the world in which we live as surely as the graceful and majestic swan is in the "ugly duckling" and the beautiful Easter lily is in its bud. May God give us the grace to let that promise bloom in us.